Wolverine

A Children Pictures Book About Wolverine With Fun Wolverine Facts and Photos For Kids

By: Alma Ray

Alma Ray

Copyright © 2016 by Alma Ray

All rights reserved

No part of this book may be used or reproduced in any manner whatsoever without the express written permission of the publisher except for the use of brief quotations in a book review. Image Credits: Royalty free images reproduced under license from various stock image repositories. Under a creative commons licenses.

I am a wolverine.

I am a large land weasel also called skunk bear.

I am related to ferrets and badgers.

I have a rounded head, small eyes and ears, short legs, and bushy tail.

I have a thick fur coat that can keep me warm in snow.

My fur can be brown or black, and sometimes with ivory stripes.

I can live for about 7-12 years.

I eat berries, squirrels, rabbits, few kinds of deer and smaller pups of wolves and foxes, even the bones.

I sometimes steal food from other animals.

I am also called a glutton because I always eat.

I can look like a bear cub.

I am not scared of fighting bears and wolves.

I can live in cold areas like the arctic.

I need a big home area to hunt and live in.

I release a bad smell to protect my home and against enemies.

I have claws that I use to climb trees and cliffs.

I can be dangerous to people who enter my home area.

I have been seen as the human superhero Wolverine.

A male wolverine is bigger than a female wolverine.

A female wolverine burrows in the snow and gives birth to 1-2 kits.

I hope you learned about the wonders of my family!

Thanks.

Made in the USA
San Bernardino, CA
14 January 2017